Falling for
Marilyn

Falling for
Marilyn

The Lost
Niagara Collection

JOCK CARROLL

FRIEDMAN/FAIRFAX
PUBLISHERS

A FRIEDMAN/FAIRFAX BOOK

Published by arrangement with Stoddart Publishing Co. Limited, 34 Lesmill Road, Toronto,
Canada M3B 2T6.

Library of Congress Cataloging-in-Publication data available
upon request.

ISBN 1-56799-411-3

Editor for Friedman/Fairfax: Sharyn Rosart
Book design: Andrew Smith
Jacket design: Jeff Batzli

Printed and bound in Hong Kong

For bulk purchases and special sales, please contact:
Friedman/Fairfax Publishers
Attention: Sales Department
15 West 26th Street
New York, New York 10010
212/685-6610   FAX 212/685-1307

Visit the Friedman/Fairfax Website:
http://www.webcom.com/friedman

In memory of Jock Carroll (1919–1995), a photographer
of many parts: clever wordsmith, avid reader, serious golfer,
patient listener, whimsical antique collector, and sharp
wit — qualities that encouraged his subjects to confide in him.
Marilyn was no exception.

IT WAS THURSDAY, JUNE 5, 1952 — OVER FORTY YEARS AGO. HARRY Truman was president, the Cold War had escalated into the Korean War, the United States had set off its first nuclear bomb, and the popular songs of the year were "Kisses Sweeter Than Wine" and Hoagy Carmichael's version of "In the Cool, Cool, Cool of the Evening."

I was about to have lunch with Marilyn Monroe.

A few days earlier, Marilyn had descended on Niagara Falls, Ontario, with a film crew of sixty, which included actors Joseph Cotten, Jean Peters, and Casey Adams, and famous film director Henry Hathaway. They had come to make the film *Niagara*.

At my elbow a chubby film publicity man named Frank Neill was on the phone to Marilyn, arranging a lunch for the Rainbow Room in the General Brock Hotel overlooking the Falls.

I heard him say, "All right, honey. He's here to do a photo spread for *Weekend Magazine*. That's the biggest publication in Canada. Fine, honey. We'll wait for you at the top of the elevator."

Hanging up, Neill turned to me. "She says she'll come right up. But that may mean one hour or two hours." He shook his head. "God knows what she'll be wearing. Here's somebody who's potentially one of the richest women in Hollywood, and she's arrived here with practically no clothes. No clothes, but lots of books. Still, she handles herself well."

He jumped up. "Look, boss, I'll go arrange a table. You guard the elevator. I'll be right back."

He'd taken to calling me "boss" in mock recognition of his publicity duties in shepherding me around the set and arranging time for me with Marilyn.

My assignment was to do a picture spread on Marilyn, a job that was to stretch into weeks, during which I would take nearly four hundred photos.

"What's she like?" I asked.

Neill said, "Boss, you're going to love this doll. All men do."

"And women don't?"

He laughed. "Some of them. And for obvious reasons."

My hasty research had led me to expect a typical Hollywood starlet, a blonde model trying to make it in movies. Her movie career had been up and down, and some of her walk-on parts had ended up on the cutting room floor. Recently she had shot to national attention with the revelation that she had once posed in the nude for a calendar photo. In those days that was big news. The calendar was selling like wildfire.

But I was not to meet a typical starlet. Completely unaware, I was walking in on the beginnings of the Marilyn Monroe legend.

Within ten years Marilyn would be found dead, apparently from an overdose of sleeping pills. In her short life she would marry a famous ball player, Joe DiMaggio; divorce him to marry a famous playwright, Arthur Miller; and become a friend of President Kennedy.

She would make such hit movies as *The Seven Year Itch*, *Gentlemen Prefer Blondes*, and *Some Like It Hot*, and share the screen with such stars as Cary Grant, Sir Laurence Olivier, and Clark Gable.

Despite fame and money, or perhaps because of them, happiness would elude her. Her hopes for a loving marriage and children of her own came to naught. Her dreams of becoming a serious actress, even a writer, would also fail, and she would be exploited as the "Sex Goddess" of the western world.

My brief encounter with Marilyn Monroe would lead me to try something new. Over the next few years I would spend my spare time writing a comic novel, a black comedy about a movie queen who came to a tragic end because of the pressures on her life. The story was told through the eyes of a naive young magazine photographer, which I was at the time.

This novel was originally published in Paris by Olympia Press, which was then publishing Nabokov's *Lolita* and the banned books of Henry Miller, Lawrence Durrell, J. P. Donleavy, and others. It worked its way back to the United States and a dozen other countries under the title *The Shy Photographer*, selling close to a million copies.

Frank Neill, the publicity man, returned to wait for Marilyn with me at the elevator. Neill had been a young reporter on a famous old U.S. newspaper, the New Orleans *Times-Picayune*, a legendary paper in the Front Page tradition. Broke reporters lowered their typewriters out of the office window to hock them until payday. Eccentric writers and editors kept bottles in their desk, slept in the city room, or served as "public relations counselors" for the many New Orleans whorehouses.

"One of the older men got me my first piece of ass," said Neill, somewhat wistfully. "For free. And from the madam herself."

Neill was still telling stories about the newspaper and film worlds when, about an hour later, Marilyn emerged from the elevator. She was wearing a white turtleneck sweater and checkered slacks.

Neill introduced me. Marilyn said hello, extended her hand, and smiled at me. What a smile. Full, red lips, white teeth, those wide-set innocent blue eyes.

When she smiled, tiny laughter lines formed at the corners of her eyes; when she looked directly at you, it made you feel as though the two of you were sharing some naughty secret. The effect on me was cataclysmic.

Less than a month before, I had spent my honeymoon in the General Brock hotel. Now her smile had sent a disturbing thought flickering through my mind. *Well, so much for monogamy.*

Neill led the way to an excellent table overlooking the Falls. Marilyn looked for a minute, then asked, "Is it true a lot of people throw themselves over the Falls?"

"Sometimes it's one or two a week," I said. I'd read it somewhere.

Marilyn frowned and turned her attention to the menu.

"I can't eat fish," she announced. "When I was a child, I couldn't even eat chicken. I would look at a leg, then I would imagine the whole animal and I just couldn't eat. I think I'll have a salad and maybe a sherbet."

I was still fumbling for words and blurted out, "I can't get over how young you look."

Marilyn's press releases sometimes described her as twenty-four, sometimes twenty-two. Actually, she was twenty-six, born on June 1, 1926. She was in the prime of life.

"I look younger," said Marilyn, "because I'm not wearing much make-up. Just like at the hospital when I had my appendix out a month ago. The nurses kept popping in and saying, 'Why, she looks like a kid of sixteen.' I remember one big, stout nurse came striding in and she growled, 'Hell — what's so menacing about you!'"

Marilyn had a publicity tour coming up for the troops in Korea and when she learned I had been there the year before as a war correspondent, she was very interested in what I could tell her. Apart from that, I was having trouble coming up with intelligent questions.

"What do you do with your spare time?" I asked.

Marilyn smiled. "Well, I've made four pictures without a break. Except for the appendix, which wasn't much of a break. When shooting allows it, I go to night classes at university. Twice a week. I make a point of sitting next to this black boy. He's brilliant. If a word comes up I don't know, I poke him and he tells me what it means.

"Apart from that, I don't go out to nightclubs. I don't go out much at all — even to premieres. The studio made a fuss when I wouldn't go to the premiere of *All About Eve*. They said it was a must. But they got over it. Sometimes, after putting in a good day's work, I can enjoy a glass of wine with friends. But I can't force myself into that sort of thing. And of course I read a lot."

"What are you reading now?"

"I'm reading *The Thinking Body* by Mabel Ellsworth Todd. And I've just finished *Letters to a Young Poet* by Rainer Maria Rilke. I read *The Prophet*. And I love Whitman and Thomas Wolfe." She looked at me. "What do *you* think of Wolfe?"

Flustered, I replied, "Well, I think he's a great subjective writer. Maybe somewhat undisciplined. I read that he turns in million-word manuscripts and that his editor, Maxwell Perkins, has to cut them in half in order to get them to book size."

"You'd understand all that," said Marilyn, "if you read his book *How to Write a Novel*. I've just finished it."

Perhaps thinking that I would get lost in literature, Neill addressed a question to Marilyn.

"Is it true what you said to Hathaway about the calendar?"

Marilyn laughed. "Yes, it's true. But it wasn't Hathaway."

She explained to me. "They keep asking if it's true I had nothing on when I posed for that calendar nude. Yesterday I said, 'Oh, no. I had the radio on.'"

We all laughed. I asked, "If it wasn't Hathaway, who was it?"

"It doesn't matter," said Marilyn. "If you want to use it, give it to Hathaway." She went on. "Funny how shocked people in Hollywood were when they learned I'd posed in the nude. At one time I'd always said no when photographers asked me. But you'll do it when you get hungry enough. It was at a time when I didn't seem to have much future. I had no job and no money for the rent. I was living in the Hollywood Studio Club for Girls. I told them I'd get the rent somehow. So I phoned up Tom Kelley, and he took these two color shots — one sitting up, the other lying down. I didn't think I'd done anything wrong. His wife Natalie was there during the shooting. I earned the fifty dollars that I needed. But people were shocked when they recognized me."

The nude photo for which Marilyn was paid fifty dollars was sold by the photographer for five hundred dollars. The calendar manufacturer was reported to have made one million dollars when the calendar caught on.

Marilyn's lunch was interrupted by a procession of autograph hounds who pushed bits of paper and menus almost in her face. They all excused themselves by explaining that the autograph was not for themselves. It was always "for my little girl who's sick in the hospital" . . . "for my nephew" . . . "for my mother who is a great fan of yours."

Marilyn obliged with a smile, but she observed in an aside, "I look forward to the day when I'll be free of all this." She added somberly, "And perhaps free of depression."

As it was becoming almost impossible to talk, Neill called for the check and we left the Rainbow Room.

★

For the next several days I dogged Marilyn's footsteps around the set of *Niagara* with a couple of Leica cameras around my neck. Picture opportunities were few but I came to be accepted as part of the scenery by the crew and, more importantly, by Marilyn.

One afternoon I accompanied her on a publicity tour put on for local officials. She made presentations, posed for group photos, and did a dutiful tour of a local factory. Marilyn brightened up my factory photos by loosening the straps of her blouse, leaning over a piece of machinery to give my camera a good view of her breasts, and flashing her best smile.

During a break on another day, she pressed me into service as a stand-in for Joe DiMaggio. A clothing shop in the lobby of the General Brock carried a stock of fine British woolens. Marilyn had decided she wanted to send a cashmere sweater to Joe in New York and she determined I was about his shape and size.

For an hour I tried on sweaters for her until she picked the one she wanted. She then disappeared to have it wrapped.

I assumed that was all I would see of her that day, but at about ten o'clock that night, my phone rang and I recognized her voice.

"About the sweater," she said. "If I mail it here, it'll have to go through customs and take days to get there. But I've discovered that if I get it to the airport in Niagara Falls, New York, Joe can have it tomorrow. But I have to get over there before midnight. Would you mind driving me over the border?"

I had my car at the front door of the hotel in short order. This time I didn't have to wait for her. But when we were waved over by customs at the Rainbow Bridge I had a moment of panic. I'd forgotten I had a case of beer in the trunk of my car, and I saw myself being arrested for trying to smuggle a case of beer or Joe DiMaggio's sweater into the United States.

I tried to stammer out an explanation to the customs man, but I was ignored. He was mesmerized by Marilyn, who was giving him her full attention.

"We'll just consider your beer and Miss Monroe as free goods," he said. And waved us on.

★

One day Neill arrived at my room with news. "Marilyn isn't shooting today," he said, "and she says she'll go out with you for some color shots after she's through with her hairdresser and makeup man."

On our way to Room 801, which was Marilyn's room, Neill said, "She likes you. Because you're taking time to get to know her."

Neill seemed to think this was cleverness on my part, whereas it was simply my lack of experience.

Inside Room 801 we found Marilyn with both her hairdresser and makeup man. The hairdresser was a petite woman named Lillian Ugrin; the makeup artist was a muscular man named Allan Snyder.

"We have nicknames for nearly everyone," said Marilyn. "Frank, here, we call Butterball, because he's so roly-poly. Lillian we call Peanuts because she's so small. And Allan we call Whitey — because he wears a white coat."

They all laughed and I gathered this was an inside joke.

"What's your nickname?" I asked Marilyn.

Whitey volunteered, "We call her AC–DC."

"AC–DC?" I puzzled. "What's that mean?"

"I don't know," said Marilyn, with her most innocent look. "I thought it was an electrical term."

Marilyn disappeared into her bathroom and Peanuts sighed with admiration. "Anybody who knocks that is just jealous."

The hairdresser and Neill departed for other duties, and I was left with Marilyn and Whitey, who began laying out his makeup jars on Marilyn's dresser.

She settled in a chair with a towel around her shoulders, and said, "Whitey's mad at me today, aren't you, Whitey?"

She explained. "I cried on the set yesterday, my mascara ran, and Whitey had to do my eyes all over again."

"There were no tears in the script," said Whitey. "If there had been tears in the script, I would have used the waterproof mascara in the first place."

He went to work on Marilyn's face. Some time later the phone rang. "It's New York calling," said Marilyn. Whitey and I knew this meant Joe DiMaggio so we discreetly withdrew to the hotel corridor.

Whitey liked Marilyn and began talking about her. "She takes life pretty seriously. Have you noticed while she's sitting around on the set, she always has a script in her hands? Well, she's not studying her lines. No, she has one of those deep soul books hidden in the script. Rilke, Franck, Freud, or maybe Emerson. She finds something in a book she thinks is true and she writes herself a little note about it. You know, 'You don't save souls in bunches,' or, 'All life is a road of discovery leading to yourself.' That sort of thing.

"She wants to be right, all the time. They don't have much of a life, you know. Reporters or photographers all the time. If they go out in public, a crowd gathers. I wouldn't want it."

Marilyn let us back into her room and began skipping about like a little girl.

"I'm going to New York for the weekend!" she cried. "If Hathaway will let me!"

She put in a call to the director and, while waiting for him to call back, ran around the room picking up clothes and a little hat and holding them against her while she examined herself in the mirror.

She groaned. "I haven't got a thing with me — just slacks and a skirt. When they said Canada, I thought it would be up in the mountains some-where. Jean Peters lent me this suit — but it doesn't fit around the hips, does it? Maybe Wardrobe will have something."

The phone rang.

She dumped the clothes on the bed and grabbed the phone, talking excitedly. She made another call. She talked more, her voice gradually rising.

When she put down the phone, she said, "They're passing the buck. Hathaway says I can leave if the unit manager says I can. The unit manager says it's all right with him, but Hathaway will have to take the responsibility. Neither of them will. And they promised before that I could go if I didn't have scenes coming up."

She sat down and Whitey began working on her face again.

"Whitey," she asked, "do you think I'm being unreasonable?"

Whitey shook his head.

"Don't say so," said Marilyn, "if you think I am. I haven't had any time off for the past four pictures."

"I don't think you're unreasonable," Whitey replied. "But, on the other hand, I didn't think they'd let you go, either. If the weather's bad tomorrow, they'll have to shoot indoors and they'll need you."

Marilyn went to the phone again. "I'll have to put in another call to Joe and tell him they won't let me come."

When the call came through Whitey and I trooped outside once more, but this time we could hear her voice through the door.

"But darling! They won't *let* me come! Don't you understand? Don't you believe me, darling?" Her voice was distraught. "But, Joe —"

The call ended abruptly as though Joe had slammed down the phone. It was a long ten-minute wait before Marilyn opened her door again. Her eyes were wet and her mascara had run.

She sat down in front of the mirror and looked at herself. She managed a kind of smile.

"I'm sorry, Whitey, but I guess you'll have to do my eyes over again. Maybe you better use that waterproof mascara all the time."

By the time Whitey had repaired her face the afternoon had almost gone, but Marilyn said we should take our planned drive. It was a beautiful sunny afternoon and I drove around the Niagara peninsula looking for a haystack. I had some naive idea that I needed one as a backdrop for a color photo. We couldn't find a haystack and in retrospect I realize I should have just stopped anywhere and photographed her against a rail fence, a barn, a field of grain. She didn't need a backdrop.

After a while I looked over and saw that Marilyn had fallen asleep, curled up in the front seat beside me. I didn't have the heart to pursue the project any more that day and drove her back to the hotel. She walked barefoot up the front steps of the hotel, carrying her shoes in her hand. I grabbed a shot of that.

When I had parked my car and returned, the hotel doorman called me over. He was almost beside himself with delight.

"When you let her out of your car and she came in barefoot, she stopped in front of my desk to put on her shoes. When she bent over *one of them fell right out!*" The doorman, at least, had had a good day.

Later that evening Neill caught up with me. "Well," he asked, "have you or haven't you? You have to admit I gave you every opportunity today."

I began to explain that it hadn't been that kind of day, but he thought I was evading the question and interrupted me.

"Okay," he said, "you're not going to talk. Probably just as well. A good friend of mine with Associated Press was banging Rita Hayworth regularly. When Zanuck [head of Twentieth Century-Fox] found out, he had him barred from the lot. Permanently. How did you do for pictures?"

"Two grab shots," I said. "One trying on Jean Peters' clothes. The other of her walking barefoot up the steps of the hotel."

"Well, better luck next time," said Neill. "We'll see when she's free again."

★

I was having some success in getting candid shots of Marilyn around the set over the next few days, but little success in setting up a session for a color cover. It depended on her shooting schedule and sufficient time for her hairdresser and makeup man to prepare her for color closeups.

And there was her tendency to be late for appointments. On one particular day we had a tentative date for ten o'clock in the morning. At ten I phoned Room 801.

Marilyn answered. "Oh, I'm sorry but I'm not ready yet. You know, I don't feel well. I don't know what could have caused it. Maybe something I ate yesterday."

I was disappointed, but said, "Well, I don't want to push you into taking pictures if —"

"Oh, no," she replied. "We'll take the pictures. But say about twelve o'clock?"

"Shall I phone again at twelve or wait downstairs?"

"You can come up."

At twelve I knocked on her door. I heard her voice, saying, "I'm not ready yet. But you can come in in a few minutes."

More time passed before she opened the door. She was alone and wearing a white terry-cloth bathrobe and, so far as I could see, nothing else. As she walked into the room I saw "Sherry Netherlands Hotel" printed across the back of the robe.

Her hairdresser had apparently been and gone, for over her hair Marilyn wore a purple net of some kind.

"What on earth is that?" I asked.

"It's a maline," said Marilyn. "But I don't know how to spell it."

Beside her bed was a huge hand-lettered sign that said, "Beware of Dogs" — a gift from the cast. Marilyn posed with it. When she sat down in front of her mirror and crossed her legs, I noticed she was wearing something besides the robe. Around her ankle was a small slave bracelet holding one or two hearts.

"They say you wear your heart on your sleeve," said Marilyn. "I wear mine on my ankle."

I looked around her room. Besides the sign, there were a few clothes, a small folding clock beside her bed, and a photo of Joe DiMaggio. Lots of books.

"Maybe you're reading too much," I suggested. "You'll confuse yourself."

"I don't know about that," said Marilyn. "I know lots of people who don't think much about anything. And they're just as unhappy as I am."

She busied herself with her makeup — she chatted just as easily about that as about unhappiness. She was using a base stick to darken the flesh tones of her face and chest. "The secret of a base," she said, "is to take most of it off. That's where most women go wrong." She applied witch hazel, then patted herself with tissue. "See? I'm taking most of it off.

"Some women work hard on their appearance. Very high fashion. I think you can go too far. You begin to dress for other women. That's why they criticize my clothes. I dress for men."

"They say some women don't like you."

"I know," said Marilyn. "You can tell these women. They keep saying, 'Oh, you're so *young*, darling!' After they've told you you're so young a few times, you know it isn't a compliment. I guess age has something to do with it.

"Here's a story you can't use," she continued. "About Zsa Zsa Gabor. She is considerably older, you know, older than anyone knows. While we were shooting *All About Eve*, she told her husband George Saunders that he wasn't to have any pictures taken with me or even talk to me on the set. But one day George had lunch with me in the commissary. He got a phone call at the table from Zsa Zsa. She said to George, 'You're having lunch with Marilyn. Now get up right away and leave the table immediately.'"

"And did he?" I asked.

"Yes, he did. I guess — you know she got a million dollars or more from Hilton, her last husband. And George — I think he says he likes the way he's living."

She was now patting on another preparation. "This is a lighter base," she said. "Better not mention it. You can end up a mess. Each face requires a different treatment."

She laughed. "I'm just giving you the benefit of Whitey. He left me a list of instructions."

I picked up one of her books. It was *The Thinking Body*. "What's this about?"

"About relaxing, partly. When you're sitting, standing — even jogging."

She stood up and began jogging up and down the room. "Like this," she said. She let her wrists go limp and her arms fly about. Inside her white robe other parts of that marvelous body jiggled and jounced around. I was so totally stunned by all this activity I didn't even think to raise my camera. I realized later that it would have been useless. I would have needed a motion picture camera to record this memorable performance. In slow motion.

Marilyn returned to her mirror. "Speaking of relaxation, I went to a Yoga church for a while. They teach complete relaxation, and there are a lot of good things in it. But I don't go for complete nirvana. They finally reach a state of desired nothing. Not now. I hope to reach that stage when I'm old, maybe.

"When I was a girl they used to call me 'String Bean,'" she said, switching topics. "I was so tall in class pictures I had to stand behind the boys."

She began to comb out her hair. I had heard her described as a platinum blonde but her hair seemed more of a golden color.

"Yes," she said, "but that's just for the Technicolor in this picture. Ordinarily it's more silver. Now it's a kind of honey blonde."

Marilyn stopped putting on her makeup and stared quietly out the window for a good five minutes. She had apparently been thinking about her childhood, for somewhat irrelevantly she asked, "Was it Freud who said that parents are the psychological murderers of their children?"

Marilyn's childhood had been an unhappy one: a father who disappeared before she was born; a mother she barely knew, who was hospitalized for mental illness; an orphanage; a series of foster homes, one run by religious fanatics and another where she was molested by an elderly boarder who gave her a nickel "not to tell." When she told, she was punished — for telling a lie.

Today, Marilyn chose to dwell on some of the happier moments. "I didn't have much school, you know. I remember in mathematics I used to write down figures, just any figures, instead of trying to do the questions. I used to think it was a waste of my brain, using it up with mathematics, when I could be imagining all sorts of wonderful things. It was so boring, such a waste. I didn't know what the word boring meant, but I knew the feeling. I used to dream I was a princess, that I could select any husband I wanted. Instead, I chose to travel around the country, disguised as a poor girl, leaving the king and queen at home, to find the man I really loved.

"He always turned out to be a poor man. Other times I used to imagine that Clark Gable was my father and that Jeanette MacDonald was my mother. They loved me very much. They used to buy me coloring books and paper dolls and pencil boxes. I had so many that I would dream of giving them away to poor girls.

"I used to like paper dolls, especially because when I was cutting them I used to make up a play about them. I would talk as the mother doll and then drop my voice and talk as the father doll. People would listen and say, 'Where does she get all this stuff?'"

Marilyn laughed. "The father doll was always constantly unfaithful and there would be tragic and mysterious deaths."

She returned to her makeup, applying eye shadow to the top of her eyelids and a soft pastel lipstick from a small jar. She fastened on false eyelashes, half-length, extending from the middle of her eyes to the outer edge.

"Later on," said Marilyn, "we had a literature assignment to write about impressions on Mexico. Instead I wrote a short story called 'Carlos — He Sleeps.' It was about a lonely little Mexican girl named Juanita who married Carlos. After that she worked in the fields, did the laundry and the cooking, and had children. Carlos, he just slept in the sun.

"One day in class, the teacher announced, 'I want to read you all something. And I want you to know that I'm amazed this has come from one of my students.'

"He began to read. I was dreaming away, as usual, not paying much attention, but then suddenly I realized he was reading my story about Carlos and Juanita. Afterwards, he said, 'Someday, Marilyn, you will be a writer.' And he gave me a list of books I should read. I haven't done much writing lately, except some poetry."

As I was making notes, Marilyn said, "I'll just give you the last verse of one. The rest is too personal."

She recited:

O, Time
Be kind.
Help this weary being
To forget what is sad to remember.
Loose my loneliness,
Ease my mind,
While you eat my flesh.

It was my turn to fall silent.

Marilyn added, "I was born under the sign of Gemini, the sign of the intellectual. But I'm definitely not intellectual. Hathaway says, 'What you do, Marilyn, you do instinctively.' It's true. I have feelings for things. I sense things. To settle for what you think is right always comes first. To get rid of my voice and my body, and then see what happens, is my ambition."

"Don't get rid of that body," I said.

Marilyn laughed. "Well, not in that sense. I told you I was a Gemini and I got a letter from an astrologer last week that will tell you what I'm really like."

She rummaged through some papers on her table and came up with a letter, which she began to read. " 'You are truly unconventional, nonconforming, and independent, an individualist, you like the strange and the curious and the original.'

"Now this part's for you. He goes on to say that most of the column items and feature writers' observations about me are such rubbish. So provincially stupid." She continued to read. " 'The biggest thing about you' — listen to this — 'is your eyes, sensitive, searching — of the beauty and goodness of pain and anxiety. Eleanor Duse had the same kind of melancholy magic in her eyes.'

"*Duse*," she laughed. "Of course this fellow wants my business. He wants me to subscribe to his service."

Marilyn finished her makeup and disappeared into the bathroom to shed her maline and white robe. She reappeared in slacks and a low-cut red blouse that buttoned up the back, but was undone.

Turning around, she said, "Do me up the back." This I managed, with some fumbling.

Marilyn propped herself up on her bed. "I know what," she said, "I have to learn to smoke a cigarette for my next picture. Give me a cigarette and you can take pictures of me practicing.

"Now this is my French inhale," she demonstrated. "Here's how I roll the cigarette from one side of my mouth to the other with my tongue."

She ran through pose after pose and I shot off a whole roll of film. For the final picture she leaned forward directly into the camera — and winked one eye.

As we finished, there was a knock at the door. I opened it and found Frank Neill in an excited state. He looked at my cameras and before entering he muttered to me in an aside, "Boss, we got a big deal going. Don't screw this up."

Having no intention of screwing anything up, I retreated to a chair in the corner of the room.

Alive with excitement, Neill turned to Marilyn. "Honey, we got a real good break. Hy Gardner wants to use you on his coast-to-coast show tonight. Along with Vice President Barkley. He's going to phone here now and tape an interview."

"All right, Butterball," said Marilyn. "But you talk to him first and find out what questions he's going to ask me. I don't want him to ask questions about Joe."

"Fine, honey."

Neill picked up her phone and sat down on the bed beside her. It took some time for Neill to get through to New York and the connection was apparently not very good because eventually he was shouting.

"HELLO? HY? IS THAT YOU, HY? THIS IS FRANK NEILL. NEILL! NEILL! I WAS JUST TALKING TO YOU ABOUT MONROE. SHE WANTS ME TO ASK YOU ABOUT THE QUESTIONS YOU WANT TO ASK HER. YOU WANT TO ASK HER ABOUT WHAT? LOOK, HY, THAT'S WHAT SHE DOESN'T WANT TO TALK ABOUT. YES . . . YES . . . YES . . . I AGREE WITH YOU, HY. I'M JUST TELLING YOU WHAT SHE SAYS. YES. OKAY. I'LL ASK HER AGAIN."

Neill put his hand over the mouthpiece. "Honey, he says this thing between you and Joe is the hottest thing in New York —"

"I don't care, Butterball," said Marilyn. "I don't care! After all, this is my personal life. And I know Joe wouldn't like it. If he wants to mention Joe's name, I won't do it, that's all."

Neil removed his hand from the mouthpiece. "HELLO, HY? LOOK, HY, MARILYN DOESN'T WANT . . . YES . . . YES. DON'T THINK I DON'T UNDERSTAND THAT, HY. I AGREE WITH YOU BUT . . . OKAY, I'LL ASK HER."

He covered the phone again. "Will you talk about baseball?"

"Sure. I'll talk about baseball."

Marilyn crouched on the bed and put her head beside Neill's ear so she could overhear Hy Gardner's voice.

"HY? YES, BASEBALL IS OKAY, HY. WHAT? . . . YES. JUST A MINUTE."

He spoke to Marilyn. "While you're talking about baseball, can he ask just one question about Joe?"

Marilyn shook her head back and forth. While they huddled over the phone, I took a picture. I think it was the first time I ever tried to photograph a telephone conversation.

"HY? I'M SORRY BUT MARILYN SAYS NO QUESTIONS ABOUT JOE AT ALL. SHE —"

In the lull, Marilyn appealed to me. "Don't you think I'm right? I don't want to turn my personal life into publicity. I know Joe wouldn't like it. It's not right."

Neill covered the phone again. "Can he ask you about Butch?"

Butch was DiMaggio's child by his first marriage.

Marilyn put her hand to her forehead in despair. "No. No. NO! Why does he want to drag the child into this? Doesn't he understand? Joe's wife has already named me in a legal action. It's completely unfair to everybody. My personal relationships are important to me. I don't care if it is a coast-to-coast show!"

"All right, honey. All right, honey," Neill soothed. He spoke into the phone again. "HY? NO . . . YES, I AGREE WITH YOU, HY. BUT — NO. YES . . . ALL RIGHT . . . JUST A MOMENT."

He handed the phone to Marilyn. "He wants to talk to you."

Marilyn took the phone. She listened. "Yes, I do understand." She listened some more. "I would like to help you. But not at the expense of someone else. No. All right. I'm sorry. Good-bye."

She put the phone down. "He's going to skip it. He'll get somebody else."

Neill wiped a hand over his face. "It wouldn't have hurt," he said regretfully. "It's a big show."

Marilyn became upset. "Frank!" she cried. "This is my personal life! They wouldn't ask Jean Peters about Howard Hughes! He wanted to ask me about Butch! I think that's terrible! I don't care that much about publicity! If you like I'll phone up Spyros Skouras!"

Skouras was then the czar of the movie industry.

Neill held up his hands to stem the flow of words.

"Honey, it's perfectly all right. We're only trying to look after you. Remember, you're ours now."

That was the end of picture taking for that day.

A day or two later the three of us were together again. Marilyn finished work early and there was some time for a walk around Niagara for some sight-seeing pictures.

Neill was full of ideas. "You could be buying some postcards. You'll probably want some anyway."

"No thanks," said Marilyn.

We came to some giant pay binoculars lined up along the Niagara Gorge for close-up viewing of the Falls. Neill suggested this would make a good photo.

"I'd like to take a look through them," said Marilyn, "but no photos. That's corny. Like in New York they say, 'Look up at the skyscrapers.' Do they think you've never seen a skyscraper before? I like pictures that have some warmth, some human quality to them."

After Marilyn had peered at the Falls, we continued our stroll until we came to a poster advertising the *Maid of the Mist* boat ride. The awesome cataract of Niagara has attracted tourists and daredevils and spawned many legends.

The earliest is probably that of Lelwalo, daughter of Chief Eagle Eye of the Ongiaras after whom Niagara Falls was allegedly named. Legend has it that she was chosen as the tribe's loveliest sacrifice to the cataract and that she paddled a birchbark canoe over the Falls to her death. The swirling mists rising from the Falls produce frequent rainbows, and it has also been claimed that at certain times a ghostly vision of the Indian maiden can be seen there. Appropriately, the boat that carries tourists to the base of the Falls is called the *Maid of the Mist*.

On the spur of the moment, Marilyn announced that she wanted to make the boat trip. Neill said he had another appointment and he left Marilyn and me to make our way down to the *Maid of the Mist* landing at the river's edge.

The boat trip, which takes place between the Niagara Rapids and the base of the Falls, is perhaps one of the shortest and most exciting in the world. Every fifteen minutes the small boat carries about one hundred tourists across the river to view the American Falls, then pokes its nose up into what's known as "The Shoe," the boiling cauldron of water only a few hundred feet from the base of Horseshoe Falls. For safety the boat is equipped with twin diesel engines, twin screws, and rudders, as well as a bank of storage batteries in case of generator failure.

Marilyn's arrival at the landing created a stir and attracted the attention of the captain. Most of the tourists were already attired in black oilskins for protection against the spray they would encounter.

The captain wanted to supply some special oilskins for Marilyn. "We have some fancy white ones," he said, "which we use for royalty."

"Please don't bother," Marilyn replied. "I'll use these." She wriggled into a set of the black oilskins.

The captain said, "You don't have to put the hood up until we get up into the spray."

Marilyn put the hood up anyway in an attempt at anonymity but it was already too late. The parade of autograph seekers began.

There was a delay in the scheduled departure of the boat and a photographer appeared on board and began snapping pictures of Marilyn and her fans. Within a few minutes of casting off, he gleefully reported, "Already I've signed up ten pictures at a buck apiece. They don't care if only the back of their head is in it as long as you are."

Marilyn sighed. "That explains the departure delay. I don't know how long I can stand this sort of thing."

The pressure eased as the boat cruised up past the American Falls and began inching its way toward the base of the Horseshoe Falls. From here the Falls were awe-inspiring, even a little frightening.

After a few minutes at the top, wet with spray, shaken by the violence and roar of the waters, most of the tourists, including Marilyn, seemed relieved when the boat began to fall back for the return run.

Marilyn asked the captain if it was true that many people killed themselves by going over the Falls. The captain was an expert on the matter.

"Oh, yes," he answered. "As a matter of fact, we get most of them at the *Maid of the Mist* landing. It takes about four or five days for the bodies to show up. The Falls keeps them trapped for quite a while — the water is supposed to be about two hundred feet deep right below the Falls. But they gradually work free and then there's an eddy in the river which brings them in to our landing.

"Right now," said the captain, "we're expecting the body of a man who disappeared from the Rainbow Room."

Startled, Marilyn repeated, "The Rainbow Room?"

"Yes," said the captain. "He was eating there with his wife and family but he got up from the table and never came back. They think he must have gone over the Falls."

(On June 11, 1952, a body was taken from the water at the landing. The body was tentatively identified as that of John A. Merckel. He was a salesman from Detroit who had been dining with his family in the Rainbow Room and had mysteriously disappeared.)

After the boat trip, Marilyn and I made our way back to the hotel. She was quiet for a while, then she brought up the suicide again.

"Just think," she said. "That man may have been sitting near us in the Rainbow Room. Imagine how unhappy he must have been to do a thing like that. That's an awful way to die — going over those Falls. I know this is a terrible thing to say, but if it had to happen, I wish I had been there to see it."

She seemed unable to leave the subject. "Some people shoot themselves." She put her forefinger to her temple and cocked her thumb in imitation of a pistol.

"But they don't do it properly and they just blind themselves. Then they're worse off than ever."

We both looked out over the water. "Sleeping pills are much better," she asserted.

T he setting for Marilyn's first starring role
was Niagara Falls.

M*arilyn was a magnet wherever she went.*
She paid ten cents to look at the Falls through one of the giant telescopes,
but refused to be photographed in such a pose because it was "corny."

"I want very much to be a wonderful wife and mother.
That's very important to me.
I say let it be a man's world as long as I can be a woman in it."

FROM THE AUTHOR'S INTERVIEW NOTES

"When I was on loan to United Artists, they shot my part, but after they edited the picture, the camera was mostly on my posterior. I didn't walk, I wiggled. After that, they sent me on a tour at $100 a week, places like Detroit, Milwaukee, Chicago. After they let me go, I had no job again."

FROM THE AUTHOR'S INTERVIEW NOTES

"My first contract was for one year with Twentieth Century-Fox. During that time I did five magazine covers and I had one line in a movie called Scudda Hoo, Scudda Hay. I said, 'Hello.' In the end, they cut it out of the picture. June Haver was their blonde star at the time and I think that's why they dropped me."

FROM THE AUTHOR'S INTERVIEW NOTES

"Columbia gave me a six-month contract but dropped me at the end.
I was staying in the Hollywood Studio Club for girls and I was broke.
I told them I'd get the rent somehow so I called this photographer I'd done a
beer ad for. That was when I posed nude . . . I tried to hide my face
while I was posing but people knew. They're pretty sharp."

FROM THE AUTHOR'S INTERVIEW NOTES

After six years in Hollywood, Marilyn's "Sex Goddess" persona had brought her to the brink of stardom.

*M*arilyn's universal appeal spawned a host of imitators.
But none of her bosomy rivals managed to project Marilyn's tenderness,
honesty, and intelligence.

Marilyn visited a local silverware factory in Niagara Falls, Canada, while making Niagara. Later, when her personal problems began to overwhelm her, such public relations gestures were rare.

"*One of the things I like best about men is that they're a little vulnerable.*"

FROM THE AUTHOR'S INTERVIEW NOTES

"I guess I look for freedom. Freedom from myself, even. From anything that might inhibit me, mentally or physically."

FROM THE AUTHOR'S INTERVIEW NOTES

Twenty-six and at the peak of her beauty, Marilyn willingly posed with curlers in her hair, no makeup, and a "Beware of Dogs" sign given to her by the cast.

When asked about her beauty mark
(a mole on the left cheek near her mouth), she shrugged.
"Sometimes I darken it, sometimes I don't."
About her growing fame she said, "I used to save every
little two-line clipping and paste it in a scrapbook. Now, I
put them all in boxes for storage."

"I love a natural look in pictures.
I like people with a feeling one way or another — it shows an inner life.
I like to see that there's something going on inside them."

FROM THE AUTHOR'S INTERVIEW NOTES

By the time Marilyn arrived in Niagara Falls,
she had already made brief appearances in twenty films, including The
Asphalt Jungle *(1950) and* All About Eve *(1950). After* Niagara *she made a
major musical,* Gentlemen Prefer Blondes *(1953), the box office smash that
made her a star and reduced her accessibility to press and public.*

Allan "Whitey" Snyder, Marilyn's makeup man on the
film, prepares her for a photo session outdoors.
Snyder met Marilyn at her first screen test in 1946; they
became lifelong friends.

"She wants to be right, all the time," said her
makeup man. "They don't have much of a life, you know. Reporters
or photographers all the time. If they go out in public,
a crowd gathers. I wouldn't want it."

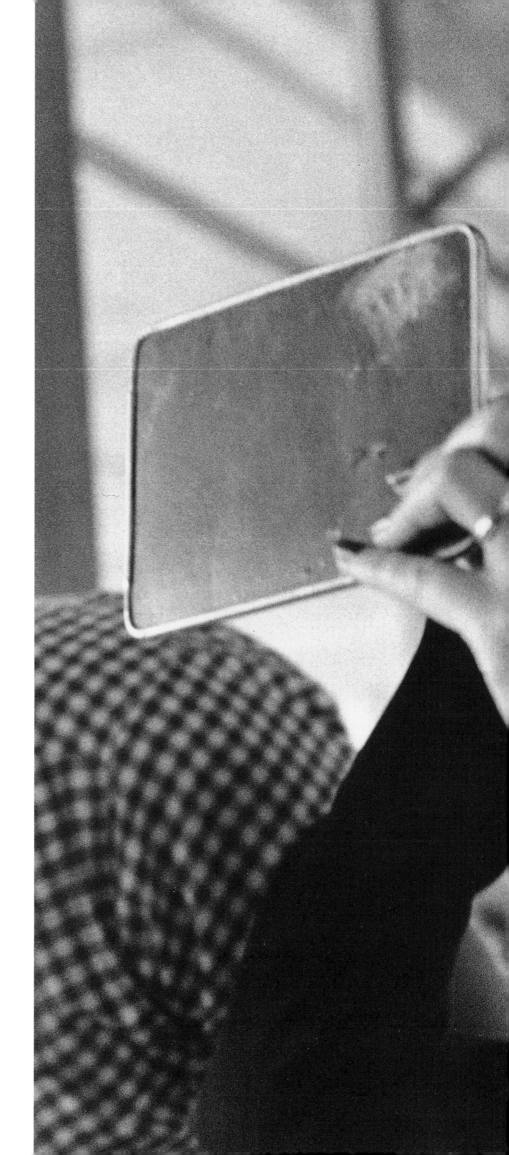

“I *want to be a real actress. I know people smile when I say it but that doesn't matter — they used to laugh at me, so I wouldn't say anything.”*

FROM THE AUTHOR'S INTERVIEW NOTES

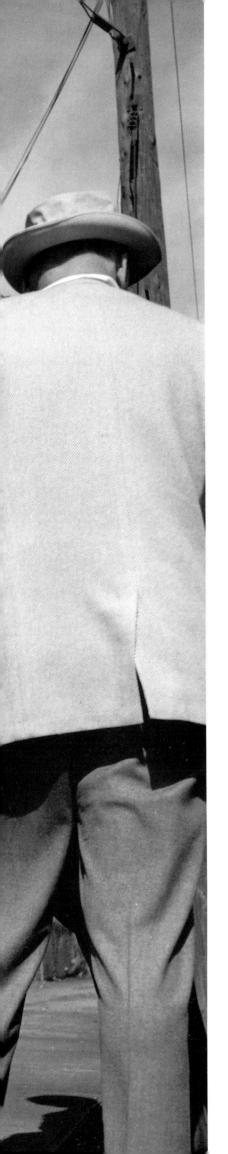

arilyn once informed an acting teacher: "I want to be an artist, not an erotic freak. I don't want to be sold to the public as a celluloid aphrodisiac."

M*arilyn was cast as a sexy dumb blonde in skin-tight outfits, a little girl who could mouth a salty remark, with eyes that projected innocence. Yet she yearned to be taken seriously.*

Marilyn shopped for clothes in Niagara Falls, Ontario, because she brought only slacks and a skirt with her. "When they said Canada, I thought it would be up in the mountains somewhere."

D*irector Henry Hathaway and Marilyn on location,*
Niagara, *at Niagara Falls, Ontario.*

H enry Hathaway gives Marilyn
directions at the bus depot, Niagara
Falls, Ontario. Marilyn got along well
with Hathaway. "Henry is very positive.
He knows exactly the way he wants
things. And everyone obeys."

FROM THE AUTHOR'S INTERVIEW NOTES

*Marilyn and co-star Joseph Cotten on location.
In the opinion of many critics, Marilyn was often paired with leading men
who were sexless freaks and mock-lotharios, and if she had played
opposite real men, she might have seemed more like a real woman.
Her performance in* The Misfits *opposite Clark Gable bears this out.*

At this point in her career, Marilyn was philosophical. "I don't feel oppressed but life is against us. Rainer Maria Rilke said something like we all choose different roads and even the closest human beings still have some distance between them. Out of that we grow."

FROM THE AUTHOR'S INTERVIEW NOTES

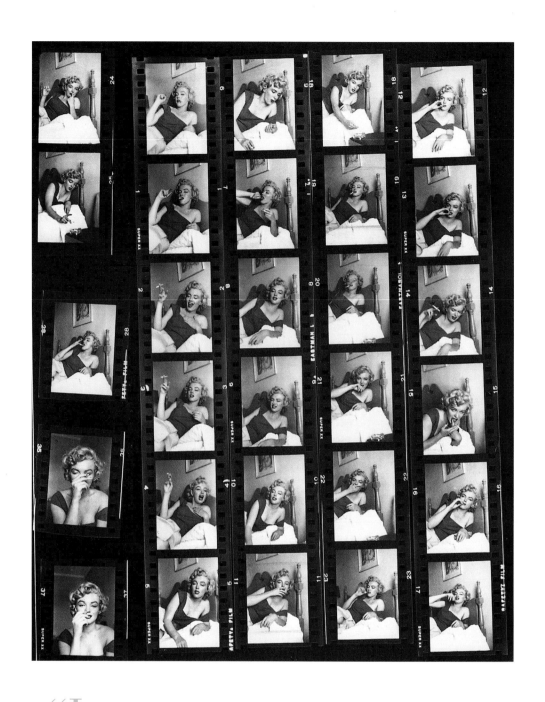

"I know what, I have to learn to smoke a cigarette for my next picture.
You can take pictures of me practicing."

After the playful posing, Marilyn leaned toward the
camera and winked. But her next remark was touchingly serious:
"I want to be — not a movie star — but a really fine actress."

FROM THE AUTHOR'S INTERVIEW NOTES

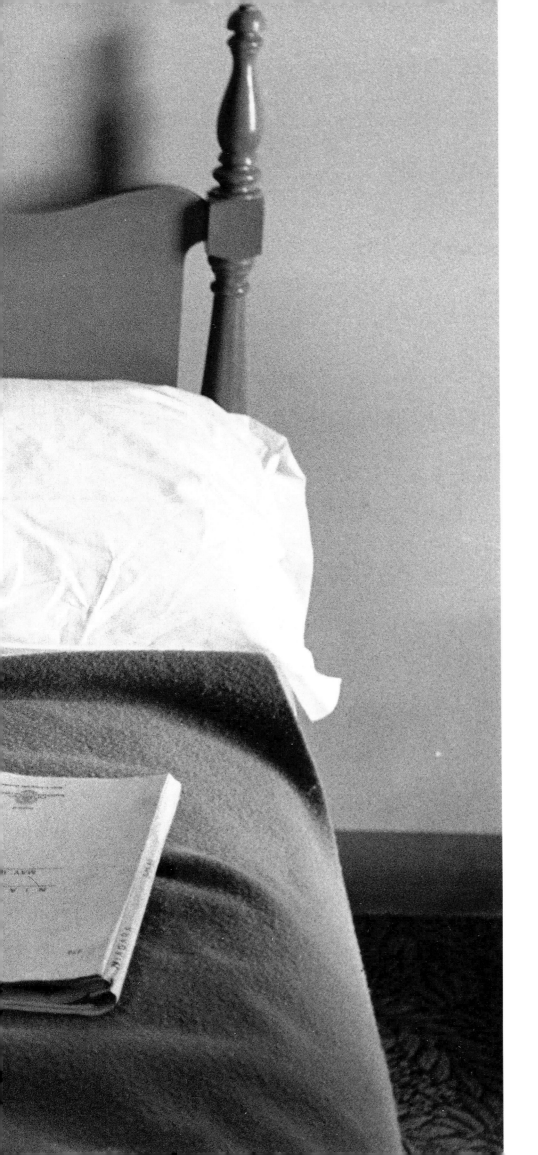

M*arilyn admired intellectuals and read constantly. She once hoped "to read all the books and find out about all the wonders . . . in the world."*

*A*nxious to get Marilyn on
Hy Gardner's show, Niagara
publicity man, Frank Neill,
tried to reach a compromise
but Marilyn refused to cave in
to pressure.

Although their marriage failed, Marilyn and Joe DiMaggio remained close. For twenty years after her death, DiMaggio sent red roses to her grave.

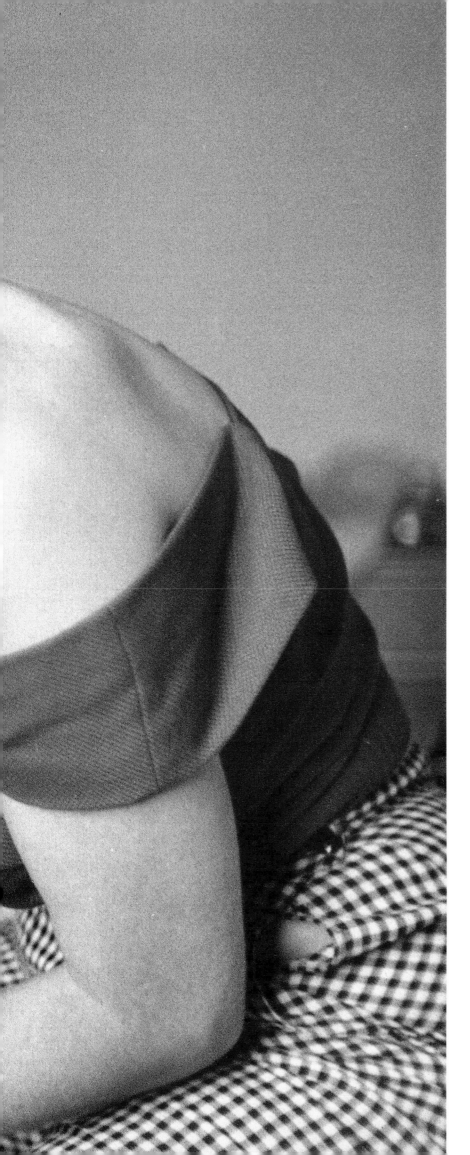

In his biography of Marilyn, Fred Guiles wrote that she was "an actress able to instill more excitement into a role than it deserved."

"Jean Peters lent me this suit — but it doesn't fit around the hips, does it? Maybe Wardrobe will have something."

A*lthough Marilyn graciously signed autographs for her fans, she longed to be able to escape the constant glare of the spotlight.*

"I was raised in an orphanage in Northern California.
My father was killed before I was born — at least they say he was killed.
As a child I had all kinds of fears and misunderstandings."

FROM THE AUTHOR'S INTERVIEW NOTES

"I want to be on the stage one day. Chaplin was a magnificent actor. Everything he does is life itself."

FROM THE AUTHOR'S INTERVIEW NOTES

In the eulogy he delivered at her funeral, Lee Strasberg said of Marilyn: "She had a luminous quality — a combination of wistfulness, radiance, yearning — that set her apart and yet made everyone wish to be a part of it."

"What a smile. Full, red lips, white teeth, those wide-set innocent blue eyes. When she looked directly at you, it made you feel as though the two of you were sharing some naughty secret."